# Mind Clutter

## Poems & Thoughts

## By Celeste Roam

*Cover Art by Matt Gibson*

# Acknowledgements

With so many great people in my life, where does one start with the thanks? Since I was a child my grandmother's writings have been a part of my life, and even though she's not here now, I believe she was a key player into my writings today. My mother and father are my biggest "cheerleaders" today in their unwavering support for me to get my poems organized to share with them and others. I appreciate all of my friends and family members who have helped through support and sacrifice to make this book possible. I couldn't, and wouldn't, have done this if it were not for others persistence in making me understand what my thoughts mean. I look forward to many years of happiness ahead and hope that I can repay all the support I have received in my adventures. Thank you to all of my loved ones, friends and family alike, and forgive my not listing you each personally as it would take a book in itself. However, I do want to give special thanks to my brother Matt Gibson for his hard work and time to make the beautiful artwork for the cover.☺

Thank you to Lago Vista Library Director, Jan Steele, for helping me meet people and educate myself on how to publish my book. Also, thank you to Lago Vista Dominos owner Ike Coronis and managers for allowing me the use of their computer to finish the details. Finally, thank you to Sandi Jossa for editing.

I would not be who I am today without each of the precious souls I've met along the way, thank you for your lessons. A special thanks to an angel on earth, Linda Bowers, and a new friend, Sydney Parks, for their donations to get the book printed. I only hope one day I will be able to repay all those that have helped me through the years.

# Introduction

Over the years my outlet in my time of need is writing. Many of the poems will be very depressing, but I was able to move on in life. I was able to avoid a common answer that a lot of people turn to. Doctors now have the answer for everything through prescriptions. I have overcome my trials through pencil and paper. I don't want anyone to read this book and feel sorry for me, or be troubled. Most people in my life currently will be shocked by the darkness I lived in for so many years, but I want to share my triumphs with others in hopes that I can shed some light in someone else's darkness, there is hope. I am not a victim; I am a survivor. I questioned at first whether to include all of the depths of my past, but realized it was necessary in order to fully understand me. My trials are what made me who I am today. I have become a confident and able person to face life without prescriptions. Depression is a difficult thing to understand if you've never been there, but many people have. I tend to wear my heart on my sleeve and have been broken hearted many times. However, I am glad for every experience I had. I would rather have 'loved and lost than to never have loved at all'. If we live in fear of heartache and judgment, then we never truly live. I don't care about judgments, because I can judge myself, we are our own biggest critics.

In my early life I felt pretty clever in my head, yet so frustrated in ways to express the thoughts. My mind is too fast, the lips too slow, and to write it all…eternity. What's in this book is my "mind clutter". It's the bits that found a way out through my hands. Some say its poetry, and some of it may be, many started as poems, but progressed to just long explanations. As I write I miss the majority of what I'm really thinking, the hand is never quick enough to get it all. It's a good way to slow me down. If there is one thing I wish would result from this book it would be that another soul that is currently troubled can find some relief in their pain. Sometimes we can feel so alone in our realities that it doesn't seem possible that anyone could understand. I do not hide from where I've been, but embrace it to help define my future. Time is always moving and so should we.

I've found more peace in my soul since I opened my mind and heart to the universe and its lessons. This does not mean my life is perfect, because I can't define perfect, but I am waiting for the lessons to unfold. I found more in life once I stopped being controlled by others judgments. An inspirational book I enjoy is The Four Agreements by Don Miguel Ruiz. Life is what we make of the situations around us. We are not perfect, we are human. The closest I can get to perfect is I admit that I am not perfect.

# Table of Contents

# Chapter 1

*Life*…
There is meaning, and I will find it

**Do you believe in destiny, or is it coincidence?**
**The secret of life, the mystery of existence.**
**The power given to you can easily be taken away.**

**Am I crazy?**
**Define the meaning of crazy…**
**Something that doesn't fit into the norm, or the masses**
**Define the meaning of normal…**
**Something that is the same as the majority and/or fits into the masses**

**What is real?**
**Do we have normal anymore?**
**Did we ever really have it?**

**Webster's Dictionary Definition:**
***crazy- adj.**
1. **out of your mind; not rational**
2. **unusual and silly**

***normal- adj.**
1. **not unusual; expected; standard**

**The sunshine of the future,**
**The shadows of the past.**
**The desire to move ahead,**
**The blindness to not look back.**
**The strength to walk away,**
**The ignorance to drop my guard.**
**The choice to try and forgive,**
**The catch whether to forget.**

**<u>Did you forget that you forgot?</u>**

**You know what you don't know, but you really don't.**
**You don't know what you don't know, or you'd know it.**
**You think you know something, when it's really nothing.**

**Normal vs Sanity vs Crazy vs Insane**
**So are we all crazy?**

## As My Universe Unfolds

As my energy begins to grow,
The darkness brings more light.
As my soul begins to see,
There's less fear in the night.
As my spirit begins to lift,
The path becomes more clear.
As my heart begins to listen,
The answers feel so near.
As my eyes begin to focus,
The world starts to change.
As my senses come back,
The goals seem in range.
As my voice begins to speak,
The secret is still untold.
As my body begins to move,
The universe will unfold.

## Re-born Each Day

See all in a new way,
start again in a new day.
Open your eyes fresh and wide,
this will be a strange ride.
Nothing as it was before,
don't look back, close the door.
The future has much to offer,
everything looks a little softer.
The surrounding essence seems,
like it's just a dream.
Another chance to get it right,
all the goals back in sight.
Attitude is a choice up to you,
you decide what to do.
Leave yesterdays pain in the past,
focus on happiness that will last.

## **Heaven vs Hell**

There can be heaven on earth
There can be hell on earth
Each day we live here
Our choices depict our reality
I saw a piece of heaven today
I saw a glimpse of hell
The love that puts you at peace
The torments life can throw you
Love is my slice of heaven
Hate is my spoonful of hell
You can't have one without the other
You need each to define the boundaries
It's difficult to hold on to heaven
It's easy to always have hell
Don't forget when you touch heaven
Try to erase the days of hell
I cherish my pieces of heaven
To give me strength to face the hell

Happiness is a collection of great moments
Sadness is a series of daily routine

## Blessing in Disguise

There's something new,
I can sense it.
I feel something hiding,
Perhaps around the corner.
I can't quite see it,
Do you feel what I feel?
My energy has changed,
Everything looks a little different.
I know where I've been,
But I know there's something else,
I will remember what I had,
But I think there's something better.
Maybe it's all just a blessing in disguise.

## A Book Not Finished

As time passes your memory grows
It's written by the decisions you chose
There's no erasing what's already been done
And the future's too short, so make it fun
If you battle your shadows brought from the past
You can cause your old problems to continue to last
The tale of your life will always be there
It's filled with people and places you shared
It's not easy when the ones close to you go
But you can't let the pain put stress in your show
You can't avoid the changes you'll face
They may just come and go without any trace
You can't predict what the blank pages will say
Anything can happen to your undeveloped day

## Today's the Day

If there were no tomorrow,
What would you do today?
Would you want to change yesterday,
Or would you be content with the past?
Have you said the things you needed to say?
Have you done the things you needed to do?
I'd jump from a plane one more time
Eat the finest food, drink the top drinks
I'd party and play, laugh and cry
Fantasies and dreams
Making love one last time
Everything you love gone tomorrow
Who would you call, or see
If today were the day?

## What You Make of It

Life is filled with ups and downs
Life is a moving rollercoaster
Life is beautiful, life is dull
Life is happiness, life is pain
Life is full of the unexpected
Life is a series of decisions
Life may have a line of fate
Life will always have many choices
Life has a chain of heart break
Life may be miserable and depressing
Life can be lit with love and magic
Life contains rainbows and sun
Life is yesterday, life is today
Life is tomorrow, the life we live
Life really comes down to just one thing
Life is what one makes of it

## A Box of Memories

It holds many things from years before
Hides many tales that are held untold
As it sits very still, its doors locked tight
You wonder what's in it, and if you're right
From dolls to books, from flowers to hooks
From clothes to kites, maybe it'll jump and bite
Who really knows what is inside?
Maybe there is nothing at all
As it mysteriously stands against the wall

## Friends

When friends leave,
They leave you with memories.
When friends leave,
They leave you feeling empty.
When friends leave,
You want to go with them.
But then there is that day,
When you open the mailbox,
And you have a letter from them.
They are never really gone,
They have left you the best thing of all,
Friendship.

## Attitude

As time keeps moving on,
I realize I'm no longer sad.
The past is the past,
And life's not all the bad.
It's all about your attitude,
It's not such a big deal.
What you truly believe in,
Is how your life will feel.

## Irony of Life

Destine in fate
Situation of coincidence
Up and back down
The waves of life
Work to live
Live to work

## Which Way?

The sunshine of the future
The shadows of the past
The desire to move ahead
The blindness to not look back
The strength to walk away
The ignorance to drop my guard
The choice to try and forgive
The catch whether to forget

## Eyes Of The New World

In our deepest pleasure,
do we know if its real?
As we evolve in our life,
will we still strike a deal?
If we strive for the new,
can we ignore the past?
Have the lessons been learned,
and will the impressions last?

---

## To Become

To become is to be,
as one grows to the light.
The stretch from darkness,
with all of ones might.
To feel the fresh air,
as we emerge into sight.
The passion is so strong,
the reward worth the fight.

---

To enjoy the new life,
one must release fear of night.
The balance is in faith,
our beliefs we hold tight.
To know harmony in life,
is to accept what is right.

## Contradiction Within

With a lot of smart steps,
There's likely stupid mistakes.
With most the cool moves,
There can be crazy reactions.
With each confident thought,
There might be a seed of doubt.
With every sensitive touch,
There's likely a heartless burn.
With all my inner light,
There is depth of darkness.
I am each and yet one,
I am nothing and yet all.

## Life and Death

Baby,
Precious, sweet
Growing, living, ageing
Marriage, alcohol, drugs, divorce
Trying, crying, dieing
Pain, lonely
Grave

## Parallel Time

Time is constant,
Time is infinite,
Time is unseen,
Time is age,
Age is growth,
Age is wisdom,
Age is history,
Age is life,
Life is living,
Life is death,
Life is uncertain,
Life is fate,
Fate is present,
Fate is future,
Fate is destiny,
Fate is time,
Time is here,
Time is now,
Time is precious,
Time is everything.

## A Deep Hate

All of a sudden it surfaced
A deep rooted pain
The love I've longed for
Full of loneliness and blame
I hate them for what they said
I hate them for what they took.
Throughout my life they stand
The coldness comes in my look
I was a child once innocent
Since I was a little they were there
I allowed them to steal my purity
Once believing they really cared
I have lost my true trust
I'm losing my beliefs and faith
I look back at my mistakes
Wondering if I'll ever be safe

## What's it for?

Will I ever understand?
Will we ever understand?
What is it all for?
Does it really matter?
Work hard to get a little,
Do nothing to lose it all.
Did I do nothing?
Or did I do it all?
When we're gone it's over,
When I'm here I'm dead.
What good does it do to care?
It will all end anyway.
But then again,
What really started?
A life of misery,
With spots of happiness.

# **Thoughts**

A shift in life
A switch in the tracks
Can't live in the past
Drop the luggage we pack
Adaptation is the way
Blending in is a need
A constant changing world
In hope we plant a seed
No definite amount of time
We all walk in some fear
Another ceiling to lie under
Time to look in the mirror

## A Taste of Life

Each day may seem the same
Same shit different day
Same job, same car
Same wanting, same needing
Is it really the same?
If you look up at the ceiling,
How many have you seen?
How many have you slept under,
Or lived under,
Made memories under?
Too many to count
Past or future
Would you consider your pallet
A taste of life,
Or always just the same?

## Expectations

Such a circle of turmoil,
Just a cloud of confusion.
Don't get your hopes up,
Just to have the bubble burst.
Looking for the support,
Just constantly to be let down.
A rift of different views,
Just an ongoing battle.
I try to grab a dream,
Just to have it snatched.
Trying to do it for myself,
Just to annoy those around.
Held to a changing standard,
Just leading to total failure.
A useless effort of energy,
Just to be sad once again.

## To Appreciate Happiness

Looking back at 2007,
now I see the stress.
A year building character,
finances become a mess.
Life can be challenging,
as the battles come and go.
Love can get us through,
even when we're low.
The sun will rise again,
another day to create.
I once lacked patience,
now I trust in fate.
I wake with new hope,
I'll have another day.
When life seems the worst,
it can't hurt to pray.

## Parental Circles

The irritation of the unseen,
the overwhelming emotions.
The feelings of utter loss,
the anger of no control.
The forever ongoing drama,
the repetitious fight.
The pressing of the boundaries,
the battle with no end.
The constant explanations,
the never ending debate.
The lack of gratitude,
the selfish expectations.
The disappointment of actions,
the painful consequences.
The desire to walk away,
the need to make it right.
The unknowing of strength left,
the "Murphy's Law" to top it off.
The frustration of understanding,
the misery of the pain.
The helplessness of discipline,
the want of healthy guidance.
The disrespect of elders,
the selfish behavior dominates.
The disregard of rules,
the blatant sassy mouth.
The losing of the mind,
the wish of shared peace.

## **Love and Hate**

Love with no boundaries
But love with rules
Someone that's always there
Yet never there at all
Live your own life
But live it for others
Seems contradictive to me
Yet makes sense to them
Just a call away
But just to be denied
If you really love me
You would support me
The decisions I make
May sometimes be wrong
I just need to be picked up
Not beaten by mistakes
Live my own life
Or I'm not living at all

## **Overload**

Work a ten-hour day
Trying to pay the way
Come home to a big mess
Not expecting any less
Milk rotting on the table
They relax watching cable
Rinse a dish, what's that?
Heaven forbid I'm a brat
I'm suppose to be the maid
And ignore as my soul fades
Just wish they'd see
A little help is the key

Do you even feel bad that the kitchen stinks?
Do you see the unrinsed dishes in the sink?
Do you know you live like a pig?
Do you care your ways make me want a cig?

## **Always Running**

The legs keep moving,
but the end is no closer.
The struggle to go faster,
what's chasing behind is nearer.
Either running to get somewhere,
or running to get away.
Is there a goal to reach,
or wanting a place to hide?
If it's not one it's the other,
sometimes it's both.
Whichever way you look,
I'm still always running.

## **A Void**

It's so empty, way down deep
In the dark depths
That hollowness
The yearning to be filled
What causes that void?
Is it the need for success?
Maybe the desire to be loved
Millions of possibilities
But there it stays
The loneliness
A rollercoaster of emotions
The void

## Dancing in the Clouds

In the performance man calls society

The show opens right where you start
People act according to their part
In the script the characters may seem the same
The masses pointing at someone to blame
The ground I walk is nothing more than a stage
Created to disguise the boundary of mans cage
The role I was given is identical to everyone's here
Designed to simplify the performance people should fear

## Walking in a Cloud

A mysterious cloak gently settles its weight
As the waves of sound freeze

## The Last Drop

My mind can't stop thinking about the ones I love
But I know these thoughts are not returned
The cold touch of loneliness is eating away inside of me
It burns in my heart as I sit by myself slowly fading
Everything I wanted has gone away and turned against me
Nothings left to fight for or even try and live for
All my energy is drained from trying to move on
But the final effort has been made and it failed

## Lies, Lies, and more Lies

Our life is set on one big lie
And no one stops to think
Is it true when you say "I do"
And it ends within just weeks
People devour gossip and secrets in lust
Even when betraying someone's loyalty and trust
We tell everyone this world is great
Not showing all the built up hate
We testify on oath in court
But some tales you just can't support
Our government tries to convince us of a world once was
No one dieing of mistakes like nuclear sludge
Just when will all these lies stop
Not until everyone is shot
So we bring in more innocent lives
That have to live with all these lies

## Losing It

Foreclosure seems inevitable
Yet few people seem to care
And to kick me while I'm down
I'm replaced for the work visa
They come over so cheap
Once mostly big co. money
Now it's spreading further
As more families sell-out
When will everyone see
We're destroying our home
America is in big danger
By their very own hands
Because greed always wins
And the good people crumble

## Loss Can = Opportunity

Work hard for someone else,
in hopes to pay the bills.
The bank moving in fast,
my sanity may need pills.
Can't afford the extra time,
like many in hope of a job.
Can I make something new,
when I feel like a blob?
Is the door that closed,
an opportunity for me?
Will a new door open,
because destiny has the key?

## Take Two

Well the end is near
And a new beginning as well
It's time to start over
Try things a different way
Will I make the same mistake?
Or did I learn the first time?
We will see in time
'Cause we're starting, take two!

## Simplicity of the World

Is the world so complex,
or is it what we make?
When you start your day,
are you happy when you wake?
As you look around you,
do you see all the gifts?
When you talk to others,
is it constantly in tiffs?
Can you stop the drama,
if things don't go just right?
As the future turns to present,
is what matters in your sight?
What is your main focus,
when your love burns in anger?
When will we all learn,
that hate equals danger?
Where will you end up,
if you're busy fighting fate?
Will you simplify your life,
before it becomes too late?

## A New Calendar

Blindly feeling the fear
As the year gets near
As the days grow less
The outcome a mere guess
Life will cease to be
What we currently see
As the solar system shifts
Existence will be a gift
Out with old and in with new
Like a fresh morning dew
Soul's dark pained nights
Replaced with peace and light
Negative needs soon past
Positive futures at last
There's anxiety in change
Things may become strange
Many could act out
Increasing violence no doubt
Humanities destiny lies
In our minds eye
Silently scared we wait
Unsure of galactic fate
Acting in love not anger
Stops revenges danger
To end energy stealing
Leads to unlimited healing
If we hold 'social mind' back
We'll know where we lack
Open our hearts to hear
Our souls have no fear

# Chapter 2

## *Drugs*...
## Is there life after drugs and addiction?

**Do you believe in addiction, or is it choice?**
**The secret of drugs, the mystery of the other side.**
**The life given to you can easily be thrown away.**

**Am I addicted?**
**Define the meaning of addicted…**
**Something you physically and/or mentally are unable to give up**
**Define the meaning of habit…**
**A repeat action in a person's routine (repeated without thinking about it)**

**Do you know that it is an addiction?**
**Can you overcome an addiction?**

**Webster's Dictionary Definition:**
***addicted- noun.**

1. **a need or habit that you cannot stop**

***habit- noun.**

1. **something that you do again and again without thinking about it**

**The sunshine of the future,**
**The shadows of the past.**
**The desire to move ahead,**
**The blindness to not look back.**
**The strength to walk away,**
**The ignorance to drop my guard.**
**The choice to try and forgive,**
**The catch whether to forget.**

**<u>Do you believe that someone can truly change?</u>**

**Are there healthy addictions?**
**Can good things come from bad habits?**
**Are you born with or do you develop an addictive personality?**

**Habit vs Addiction vs Need vs Want**
**So are we all addicts?**

## She's So Beautiful

The clouds begin to drift away
Light of a new kind glistens behind
There is clarity in my thoughts
An awakening takes place deep within
The familiar comfort sweeps through
A relaxation takes place as a whole
The feeling is like nothing else
A complete understanding is welcome
The usual anxiety slowly fades out
As the addicting ritual continues
The surrounding environment is perfect
A desire and lust is given to her
The sweet aroma and heavenly taste
The inhaling that feels so good
Do you know who she is, that love of mine?

## The Eyes of an Alternate World

**The young one that we all once knew,
The pots of temptation begin to stew.
As the journey takes an abrupt twist,
A friend awaits for your first kiss.
Now you found what the darkness hides,
Are you prepared for an exotic ride?
Curiosity tends to blind all doubt,
The entrance can't be your way out.
The enticing maze stands ahead,
Forgetting all warnings ever said.
As the virgin youth slowly steps in,
A desire spreads for the taste of sin.
Now you crave for the unknown,
Are you ready to except this as home?
The world of secrets is like a big sea,
A needing sensation feeds at a fee.
The chance of escape decline and fall,
The senses fight to feel and learn all.
As the passion for the false reality rises,
A seductive caress reflects future prizes.
Now as you look all around,
Hear the cries of new fears found.
The heart is the victim of the hit,
The tears vanish into an eternal pit.
Now your future will never be the same,
Will you beat this addicting game?
Wait a second before you cross the line,
Take another look when you think your fine.
Before you decide you are willing to play,
Be sure you know the true price you pay.
When you turn around and open your eyes,
Don't make excuses for your new world of lies.
Look closely at your reflection in the mirror,
Look past the white curtain for your new cure.
The truth you now face is not any fun,
Your inner strength will direct where you run.
The past is where your old world waits,
Do you know if it's too late?**

## Spinning Circles

The four solid boundaries keep me confined
As they move in closer to capture my mind
The support beneath becomes a moving sea
As my sense of balance drops me to my knees
The instant fall sends a shock to my head
As my thoughts spin out of control with dread
The surroundings I knew now fade away
As my direction of focus was blinded by gray
The world around me melted into an evil trap
As my days altered to a life feeding crap
The power of the change I was facing grew
As all I believed in was no longer true
The cage that contains me at first was weak
But eventually the barriers patched every leak
Unfamiliar ways put desperation in my heart
The need for saving before I fall apart
Darkness replaced areas where I'd seen light
Coldness sweeps through and chills the night
The fear intensifies in my confusing state
As the loneliness closes the chance of escape
The room before me scares me like never before
As it's spinning ground below no longer a floor

## Everything's Spinning

Our society built by the system is the base upon we stand
The circle it forms draws you in like a motherly hand
The idea of conformity is what they want us to follow
As they shelter the truth from our eyes they make hollow
The protective rules try to keep me confined
As they move in closer to capture our minds

## Where Is Everyone

I need you, where are you
Is there anyone
Each person out for themselves
No time for help
Does anyone care
I am hurting here
Do they call…yes
For me…no
Everyone looking
For something they want
Just a little honest attention
That's all I am asking
But who has time
To stop for me
Busy helping themselves
No one's really there for you
Just yourself
Am I stupid for being there
When they need me
Perhaps, 'cause where are they
When I need them

No family, No friends, No one
Just me

## Always the Same

It’s like a broken record
It’s just another re-run
I’ve seen this same show
I’ve felt just like this
Sitting once again alone
In the middle of a crowd
No one will see me
‘Cause there’re getting high
Can’t seem to get comfortable
I never can fit in
The hurt and pain hit me
Soon boiling into anger
An emotion I don’t like
In the end it all goes wrong
I’ve seen this same street
We’ve walked it before
If there is a hell
It’s eternal repetition

## Where It Can Take You

You can run, but you can not hide,
Everyone's in it, you already chose a side.
You can't close your eyes, and wish it away,
It will still be there the very next day.
You can't stop what's already begun,
It's a challenge you won't think is fun.
You must face up to the trouble you're in,
Or karma will pay you back for your sins.
You won't make it with a silly cop out,
It's time to grow up, and take the hard route.
You were never told this was going to be easy,
Swallow your pride, and quit acting queasy.
You're going to make a mistake or two,
But everyone does, no matter who.
You know that time will heal the pain,
Don't hold it in, it will drive you insane.
You may not live, if you fall in that hole,
Asking for some help, could save your soul.
You're not alone in this twisted little game,
Since your still here, what is your name?
You can't turn around and just walk away,
It's in your blood, the addiction to stay.
You thought you were "bad" at the start,
Now watch as your life falls apart.
It's too late now to call "evens" and quit,
You're gathering speed, on your way down the pit.
Prepare yourself for a few more bumps,
When you hit bottom, you become another chump.

**The Lady in the Park**

Is how you see yourself,
how everyone else sees you?
Is the person you are,
who you wanted to be?
Do you understand your direction?
Do you realize what is reality?
I once believed in a world of fantasy,
I once lived in a life of the game.
I lost everybody I loved,
I lost everything I cherished.
I forgot who I was,
and didn't see who I'd become.
And then I met her, a stranger,
with her eyes of disgust.
Her piercing look, making a mirror,
there I was, with the lady in the park.

## Tables Turn

See the world for what it is
See the people for who they are
To think and believe one thing
To know and find out another
Nothing is really how it seems
Nothing is ever what you want
I thought they liked me
I believed they loved me
Now I know it's not me
Now I found out who it is
It's not a person to trust
It's not a soul to cherish
There are other things in life
There are different things to hold
Wishing it was my heart and mind
Wishing it weren't the game and drug
The tables have turned now
The truth has always been there
Once a bond of trust and love
Now a table of distrust and pain

## Loved Ones

From my past
Most of them are gone
From my present
Most of them are leaving
For my future
I will be alone
I once had loved ones
Soon just myself
Some left while I was away
Some died when I was there
Some I watched kill themselves
Either way the end is the same

Loved ones here,
Loved ones there,
I open my eyes,
They're not anywhere.

## No One to Love, Chances Lost

As I sit alone in my room,
I find I have nothing to hold.
Rain drops play games on the window,
But I stay still in a cold silence.
As the world sheds its tears,
I look at pictures of past memories,
And listen to songs once sung.
I reminisce times I had someone,
And watched them slip and fade away.
I gave up chances once given,
And now stare at eternal loneliness.
My heart bleeds and my eyes tear,
My soul cries and the pain escapes.
But nobody's here to listen, see or care,
What wrong roads I took back then.
I am left with nothing to hold,
And no one to love.

## Where Can I Find an Exit Out?

**No matter where I go in a time of need,**
**There's a world of lies growing like weeds.**
**I try and run from the ghosts and their grins,**
**But they always appear, I'll never win.**
**The challenge keeps growing in this evil game,**
**All the problems & fights all sound the same.**
**My puzzle seems a journey meant to be endless,**
**I'm drowning in pain that's eternally mendless.**
**My mind continues to beg for a safe place to hide,**
**I'll forever search for someone true at my side.**
**My heart tries to patiently wait and not follow,**
**A persons past can leave them feeling hollow.**
**Times meant to be happy, are tears of depression,**
**Places once full of friends are now thick of tension.**
**My help and care of others has a price to pay,**
**I sit forced to watch my chances slowly slip away.**
**My heart is used and abused by souls that are lost,**
**Causing confusion of where my dreams and reality cross.**
**I can't manage to decide what is real or not,**
**My storm of emotions shadows my thoughts.**
**Fear of the truth is what people won't face,**
**Truth can be harsh and cruel despite the place.**
**I attempt to ignore how it hurts to be alive,**
**But denial is worse when I'm asked to survive.**
**There's not much for me to hold to soften the fall,**
**The stress is eating away the rest of my wall.**
**My focus has become cloudy and lost its shape,**
**An old temptation persists on the easy escape.**
**My sanity drains into an abyss of the unknown,**
**My limited time digs the pressure deeper than my bones.**
**I wish not a care or a worry could touch me in harm,**
**Instead I cover my pain from drugs evil charm.**
**Everything's become more than I can handle,**
**Soon it will blow out my spirit like a candle.**
**My goal is to open a door to get out and fast,**
**So I can enjoy a life different than the past.**
**I'm grasping tight to a couple fragile hopes,**
**Never to forget what I learned hooked on dope.**
**I promised myself to leave a message behind,**
**My memory of answers to secrets of the mind.**

## A Shell

Existing in a shell of a dead person
Not living 'cause I'm already dead
If I had the balls to kill myself
I wouldn't still be here
All emotions totally gone
All love completely slaughtered
Wishing for a one-way ticket
To the heavens above
Left alone in my little shell
Searching for a way out

## Forever Gone

Here is where I am today,
Tomorrow seems so far away.
My mind boils in thoughts not sane,
While my heart screams out in pain.
I'm scared of what I'm about to learn,
I'm crossing the line of no return.
I'm trying to remember things in my past,
Not sure if I have the strength to last.
It's all over I can't take anymore,
Please make it stop, just close the door.
Hold on this isn't what I wanted,
I'm lost in a world that is haunted.
No turning back when the choice is made,
I already feel my soul slip and fade.
Goodbye to what I once had here,
I'm all done, and I have no fear.

## No More Fears

It's time to let the feeling free
In the morning I'll be gone away
All the things I left behind

## Lost and Falling

The darkness surrounds,
And death sneaks in.
The shadows move on,
And the end begins.
The soul stands still,
And the heart pace slows.
The body follows,
And there's no place to go.
The mind is lost,
And feelings drown in despair.
The senses take their last
Breath of sweet air.

## **After Effects**

I sit here and ponder the idea of death,
I should be held responsible, but it's too much stress.
I am partly to blame for this bad deed,
I wish I had a friend in this time of need.
I can't look, or talk to my mom,
My life shattered by the devils bomb.
The look of disappointment is on her face,
As I shrivel I pray my life back in place.
If I had it to do all over again,
It wouldn't result in my deaths new begin.
Maybe the punishment will be over soon,
Never forgotten, not till a blue moon.
I've decide for now to hold on to life,
I've put down that deadly knife.

## Another Chance to Get Out

I see a fog of confusion all around,
I pause at the opportunity found.
I stumble slowly in the choices I face,
My time is running out in this life chase.
The pressure is beginning to test my will,
I'm trying to pick the path leading uphill.
Desire for my answer is burning deep,
The fear of losing, my heart still keeps.
Every loss leaves my soul with a scar,
The pain I hide is locked like a jar.
Only the mental power I hold helps me,
I feel alone in this attempt to be free.
I presently stand at the start line again,
I'll play hard till death, 'cause I must win!

# Chapter 3

## *Love...*
## Is there life after a broken heart?

**Do you believe in fate, or is it chance?**
**The secret of love, the mystery of the heart.**
**The love given to you can easily be lost.**

**Am I in love?**
**Define the meaning of love…**
**There are many kinds of love, but in general it is the feeling of pure, unconditional, and honest caring adoration for someone or something.**
**Define the meaning of hate…**
**Strong feeling of distain or disgust towards someone or something**

**What is pure?**
**Do we have honest anymore?**
**Did we ever really have it?**

**Webster's Dictionary Definition:**
***love- verb.**
1. **have a deep feeling of affection for someone**
2. **like something very much (opposite hate)**

***hate- verb.**
1. **feel strong dislike or anger (opposite love)**

**The sunshine of the future,**
**The shadows of the past.**
**The desire to move ahead,**
**The blindness to not look back.**
**The strength to walk away,**
**The ignorance to drop my guard.**
**The choice to try and forgive,**
**The catch whether to forget.**

<u>**Do you believe in love at first sight?**</u>
**Can someone be in-love with 2 people the same way at the same time?**
**Can you love someone with all your heart and hate them with every fiber of your being simultaneously?**

**Love vs Lust vs Obsession vs Infatuation**

**True love is unconditional, truly wanting the other person's happiness and well-being even if it is not with you.**

## **Affection**

The want, need, desire
The craving, lust, obsession
The mind wants it
The heart needs it
The body craves it
The emotions craving
The spirit lusting
The energy is obsessed
Staying strong to hold together
So easy to fall apart
My heart aches
For that gentle affection
The touch that puts me at ease

## Taking a Step

I see something between us, when I'm with you I glow
I'm not sure where I am, not sure where to go
There are so many questions, treading in waters unknown
I find myself going somewhere, a direction never shown
There's a comfort between us, things feel so right
There's a wall around me, and fear holds it tight
I'm scared to make a decision, afraid of what I don't know
I'm trying to take a step, still moving forward just slow
If I knew what was best, where the answers are hiding
Being pulled a million directions, inside of me pure fighting
Should I follow my head or heart, which is the way?
Everything's happening at once, in chaos it's hard to say
Only in time will we know, I don't know what I want to do
I don't want to ruin what could be, what's between me and you

## Down Deep

The things you'll never know
The feelings I can't let go
The long nights I couldn't sleep
The tears I refused to weep
The chance I dreamed for
The day you'd open that door
The words I wish you'd say
The desire that you would stay
The envy for her for what she had
The pain she caused makes me sad
The world I want to give to you
The things that you won't let me do
The love that I hold down deep inside
For someone that I will have to hide

## Who is Who?

She looks so innocent,
She seems so sweet.
Her make-up done so nice,
Her hair fixed up neat.
Her voice is very soft,
Her clothes are just right.
You think she can do no wrong,
You could never imagine a fight.
I've seen her on the inside,
The outside is what you see.
Her motives are unknown,
She'll be who you want her to be.
I know what she's doing,
I've seen it all before.
Can't you see what I see?
I could give you so much more.
She's not real or true,
She's just a kid that's fake.
Her inner-self is ugly,
Do you know what's at stake?
I know who I am,
I know what I want.
I'm so much more,
She's just a taunt.
What we had was love,
Something she thinks she knows.
She's evil and backstabbing,
It's just a game as far as she goes.
She's tearing us apart,
When will you see what I see?
You trusted me before,
It's you that holds the key.

Don’t lose your true love,
For misery and hate.
You were once happy with me,
You said I’m your soul mate.
She’s a Barbie just out of high school,
She’s not who you are looking for.
She’s lying to you already,
She’s just a bag chasing whore.
I’ve always been loyal to you,
I wanted us to have the best.
I loved you unconditionally,
Now you’ve put us to the test.
You made me promises,
That you chose not to keep,
I believed in you,
The pain in my heart runs deep.
“Little girls” are all the same,
If you lose me, you are to blame.

## Only Time Will Help

Can you hear it? It's silent--yet so loud.
The sound of something breaking.
There it is again, another piece
shatters in the darkness.
Can you feel it?
It aches and burns inside, the shock of the pain.
There is that helpless feeling as another piece
falls.
Can you see it? It's hard to believe
in what you can't see, but it's there.
It's happening right now, this isn't the first time.
Each time it's a little deeper, more broken pieces
left behind.
The sounds of the past, the feeling of being hurt,
blind by confusion.
What do you do? Do you know what it is?
The sound of silence.
The feeling of loneliness.
The sight of a broken heart.

# **Torn**

Stuck between love and freedom

Longing to go back
Wishing to move forward
To hear his voice
To see his smile
To have no rules
To feel no obligation
Wanting what we had
Excited for new things
Caught in what was said
Lost in what to do
Wearing his promise ring
Talking of other men
Two roads to take
Torn in the decision

Lovers-Friends-Nothing

## Am I Falling?

The mind and heart
Never working together
My mind tells me no
But the heart says different
The mind afraid to agree
Trying to protect the heart
As the heart beats faster
The stomach doing twists
My brain trying to make sense
Is my heart just confused?
The heart is too trusting
The mind trying to remind
Lost in the turmoil
Why can’t I walk away?
Is it true this time?
Or is my heart just falling?

## One Night

The butterflies lift one
The moment captures you
The hormones take control
The morals escape through
The passion hides the reason
The feeling meaning all
The void momentarily gone
The phones silent call
The guilt is seeping in
The idea holds till dawn
The reality hits hard
The one night is gone

## **No Hurry**

Sitting here wondering why
Knowing what I did is done
Praying and hoping I am wrong
Remembering it was all out of fun
So caught up in the moment
I knew it was best to wait
I watch the phone in its silence
The message loud, but it's too late
I recall that patience is a virtue
And love shouldn't be rushed
Never before have I just jumped in
The lesson is my heart got crushed

## Love?

Depression sets in
And the thoughts go wild
You try to let go
But the feelings increase
Lost your heart feels
Searching for true attention
Desire to be important to somebody
To know that someone is there
Reaching out with a plea
Finding only emptiness all around
Truly we are all alone
Maybe to never share another heart
Can we live like that,
And still go on?
I have and I do
Dreaming of a person who cares
Will I ever be number one with someone,
Or will I search forever alone?

## Stuck in the Middle

I’ve lost who I loved,
And love what I’ve lost.
I can’t bring you back,
And I can’t let you go.
I turn to run away,
And I turn to look for you.
I want you to hold me,
And I want you to let me go.
I’ve never felt so caged,
And I’ve never felt so free.
I’d take you either way,
But not in between.

## What Do You Want?

**Love…**
It can make you float,
It can make you fall.
**Trust…**
It can bind you together,
It can break you apart.
**Honesty…**
It can make it easier,
It can make it worse.
**Loyalty…**
It can bring you closer,
It can suffocate both.
**Compromise…**
It can make you share,
It can make you selfish.
Where do you draw the line,
so that everyone is happy?

When we fell in **love** with each other it made me float.
Our **trust** bound us together.
Our **honesty** made it easier.
Our **loyalty** brought us closer.
And **compromise** rarely needed, we were just alike.

## Back Again

The tears are beginning to fade away
The pain found in my heart I'll hold for days
He walked away like I was a stranger
Didn't look back to see if I was in any danger
He's already forgotten the feelings we shared
Or was he always pretending that he cared
He now lives a life I'm no longer a part of
I was blinded by what I thought was love
Slowly the memories will slip to the past
My life without him has started at last
Now I find myself falling back apart
He's back again confusing my heart
What does he really want from me?
Is it worth the risk to chance and see?

## The Silence

There's something you'll never understand
Something in my heart I hadn't planned
But it doesn't matter now
I wish there was a way, but how?
You accepted everything about me
But didn't give your love I now see
We were close for a short time
But I realize you will never be mine
Maybe you're afraid, maybe not
More than likely you just plain forgot
Your silence is killing me inside
Loves pain becomes harder to hide
Is it my fault I fell in love with you?
Can you forgive me, what can I do?
I'll try and move on, give you your space
I'm sorry if I got on your case
I thank you for the time we shared
Please don't forget how much I cared
I hope you remember me when you're away
I know I'll think of you every day

## Actions Speak Louder Than Words

Once again your actions
Have broken my heart
I wonder what means more
And if I mean anything
I know that you love me
But you don't really show it
Every minute of every hour
Of every day I think of you
When do you think of me?
Rush, rush, hurry, hurry
And away you go
And once again I am left
Forever waiting

## Waiting

I was waiting in his bed
But he was warm with her
I was lonely loving him
While she made him purr
I was busy missing 'us'
But the motel bed was full
I was keeping 'our' bed warm
While he just fed me bull
I was giving him my heart
But she stole his eyes
I was dreaming of our love
But he just gave me lies
I wish I hadn't been waiting
He wasn't thinking of me
She is who he wants now
Once again I didn't see

## Can a Person Change?

Once a certain way,
can you ever change?
If you do change,
are you really changing?
Is it something new,
but still just the same?
Gave up a bad habit,
and picked up another.
Then there's some,
that just never change.

## **So Many**

So many points of view,
So many senses disarray.
So many needs to leave,
So many reasons to stay.
So many feelings of love,
So many actions of pain.
So many vibes of affection,
So many thoughts not sane.
So many hopes of our future,
So many stings in our fights.
So many words of promise,
So many goals out of sight.

How can you be so right together in so many ways,
But still be so wrong?

## A Mess

**I used to see beauty on the inside**
**It made me beautiful on the outside**
**I once felt together and complete**
**I believed I was on the right path**
**Now my world is spinning**
**I'm caught in this great web**
**I blindly put myself here**
**And now see where I'm at**
**It's definitely not what I wanted**
**It's far from what I dreamed**
**There are so many pieces to pick up**
**So many choices to be made**
**I feel my life is like water**
**Slowly slipping through my fingers**
**The tighter I try to hold on**
**The faster I lose it all**
**A darkness is surrounding me**
**It grows from the hole in my heart**
**Each day it gets harder to move**
**Every moment I fear the next**
**Where there was light in my eyes**
**Now I only see black**
**What I have most would envy**
**What I've lost I can't forget**
**My heart and soul are drowning**
**My mind is going insane**
**I have little left to hold onto**
**I reach out to grasp at nothing**
**My faith in myself is damaged**
**I have no energy for repair**
**If I knew my love would leave**
**I never would have loved**
**Everything is happening at once**
**Can I sort the mess I made?**
**Can I live passed what I've lost?**
**Will I find answers through my mistakes?**

## The Beginning of the End

Every day another lie,
That I'm supposed to buy.
How can I just sit still,
It's taking all my will.
It gets harder to smile,
Being angry all the while.
I'm going totally insane,
My heart in so much pain.
Why do I bother to care,
Your happy presence so rare.
You just go when you want,
The memories will forever haunt.
I'm not here to be alone,
You won't even pick up the phone.
Go ahead and have your fun,
Don't wonder why we're done.

**Pin in the Heart**

Lies, betrayal, hidden truths
I have found all in my life
Feel the hurt, pain, anguish
Every piece shattered inside
The heart flounders in me
Grasping for the explanation
Knowing there may never be one
Trying to remove the pins
Each stabbed in the depths
Carefully attempting to remove all
A tear drop, a blood drop,
Unable to repair the damage done

## The Truth

It's what we all seek,
usually not what we want to find.
Most often we already know,
not wanting to accept it.
Then there's an icy slap,
there's no denying it.
The truth is what's real,
not where most live.
It's knocked on my door,
a painful lingering sound.
I was living in fantasy,
what I dreamt was real.
Now there's no denying it,
just the cold truth.

## **Once Again**

I get so tired
Of being here again
The face of another woman
I hope my soul will mend
The women just kept coming
The river never stopped
I kept holding on while
My heart continued to drop
I can't believe it's been so long
Since I decided to let it out
Nothing has really changed
I was trying not to doubt
I thought if I gave him a chance
Things might turn back
But here I am again
Trying to hurry up and pack

As he moves on unknowing
The love inside of me still growing
The words want to come out
But they're held in with doubt
I wish the words could be told
But to my grave I will hold
Is he blind to what I feel?
Does he even give a deal?
I try to go on, and not look back
My heart is going to have an attack
Oh what a pain he has left me
I trusted him, why didn't I see?
If only I'd listened to my mind
But no, I followed my heart blind

**Played**

He gave me happiness never known, with the right moves, and the right words.
My confidence was sent soaring; I had wings to fly with the birds
I hoped it would last forever, but my mind had its doubts.
It was a dream come true, I was soon to let it all out.
My heart had trust in him, the love was quickly growing.
The distance suddenly moved in, he walked away no regret unknowing.
I fell for him, why, if I'd listened to my mind?
He swept me off my feet, and my heart followed blind.
Will he be happy with her, as I try to not look back?
I'd treat him like a king; I think I'm having an attack.
Everything is so confusing, my world is falling apart.
Is he really gone, can't we go back to the start?
How do I get over this, maybe I should run away?
Is the trouble worth it, it's not the first time I've been played.

## Alone

So many people around,
yet nobody at all.
Life is so beautiful,
yet absolutely dreary.
I sit with an emptiness,
not sure what will fill it.
Feeling so wanted,
and yet so rejected.
It's all just a game,
but it means something to me.
Does it mean something to you,
do I mean something to you?
Sometimes I wonder,
is it real this time?
It all means something to me,
but I feel alone in this.
Nobody to share myself with,
not even a second glance.
I feel so lost and alone,
with only hope to hold me.

## Lost

Lost in a drowning world
What once was perfect
Now falling apart
Was it meant to be?
A perfect world, no
One leaving you empty
Is there love,
Or only need and desire?
Do you run away,
Or go down in what was?
Can't run far enough
Can't run fast enough
A dieing world in my heart
Forever to stay
Do I fix the problem?
Or just turn and pray?
What once was,
Will never be again

## A Broken Soul

What I thought I was
Now torn away
The eyes that pierce
The whispers that burn
Is there an escape
And where do I find it
Is there any truth
Or is life just lies
My pride is shattered
No energy left to hold
Alone I walk in dark
Wishing for that light
I almost grasped it
But it quickly fled
Am I unworthy
All the scars I bear
I'm sorry for the pain
I wonder about life
A part of me wishes
It would all just wash away

## Walls

As he walks away in the chilly night
Another wall is created
He has no idea what has happened
But she knows it's not the same
The talk was supposed to make it better
But in reality it made it worse
He is afraid of the pain once felt
She is scared of what will be
Why do the walls always have to be there?
When there are suppose to be none
Everyone hides from their fears
Is it from what was, or could be?
Each with their own reasons
Each unable to forget the past
She wants to reach out to him
But he turns from her to escape
He doesn't want to face it
And she's afraid to help
The feelings are pounding to get out
But the bars keep them locked away
Will it always be like this?
Or is there a way to break it?
That would mean letting the walls down
The big question is 'are you ready'?

## **A Change in Perception**

The picture that changes
Just turn it upside down
It's still the same picture
But it portrays something else
Is it all a matter of view?
Or is it all just the same?
I held the picture one way
My eyes looked at it another
I thought he was the one
Now I question what I saw
Maybe it was just the idea
Maybe it was really there
I spin it in all directions
Getting dizzier as I go
Then I come to a sudden stop
Realizing it was just a dream

## Who's Inside…Does Anyone Know?

I try to stand strong and ignore how I hurt,
will everyone betray me and treat me like dirt?
I'm not writing for all to read like a book,
behind my eyes is where one can look.
I'm becoming caught in problems others made,
I don't want to be part in this game being played.
Can people be honest in what they say and do?
Give me a chance, I'll trade a promise that's true.
Forgive and forget is a phrase many don't know,
life is short, is getting revenge the wise way to go?
Please take some time to search a soul deep inside,
most likely you'll see through the walls where people hide.
I'll open myself and show the truth to those that ask,
otherwise I must protect myself with society's made mask.
Everyone today carries a heart they made harder to find,
'cause it gets tangled and lost in battling games of the mind.
To be a friend you risk pain by offering trust,
if you trust me I'll be there 'til I'm dust.

## Life Goes On

I wonder what it could be like,
but the road just keeps on turning.
If only I could stop it all,
and get rid of the burning.
My heart held onto a dream,
just to be let down again.
I saw it all coming before,
I must keep my thoughts sane.
The shadow over his heart,
the sorrow that's in mine.
I hope she makes him happy,
I see such a fine line.
What I was wishing for,
it will soon be all gone.
I love him so much,
but my life must go on.

## **Set Free**

A bird with wet wings,
can not fly.
I will dry your wings,
So you can go.
My wings are drying,
But we will part.
I miss what we shared,
There's a whole world ahead.
I wish we could fly together,
But we are a different kind.
The taste of freedom,
No rules or obligation.
I can feel the beginning,
No more of the past.
I will be free,
Just wait and see!

## Perfect?

He makes my stomach turn,
He makes my heart ache.
I wish I could be with him,
Instead I'm forced to be fake.
We share magic when we're together,
I wonder why we can't be.
He's what I wish I was,
I dream one day he'll see.
It obviously won't work,
Why must my heart fall?
The timing isn't right,
Perfect…it's not at all.

## A Passing in Time

There he was,
There he goes
I held him close,
I let him go.
I helped him see,
What just couldn't be!

## Wandering

Wandering through life,
Another thought flits in.
Another ceiling to sleep under,
Another day passes by.
I've laid my head lots of places,
I've watched people move on.
I've met many souls,
I've loved many hearts.
I long for what I had,
I dream for what I'll get.
But presently I walk,
I'm still just wandering.

# Chapter 4

## *Dedications*…

Poems dedicated to loved ones

Do you believe in family?
The secret of life is to love everyone.
The time we share with family and loved ones should be cherished,
because you don't know how long you have.

The sunshine of the future,
The shadows of the past.
The desire to move ahead,
The blindness to not look back.
The strength to walk away,
The ignorance to drop my guard.
The choice to try and forgive,
The catch whether to forget.

Treat others like you want to be treated.
Always say I love you whenever you can, it may be the last time you say it to that person.
Learn to forgive others, because others have forgiven you.
Always base your actions on love.

Family vs Friends vs Acquaintances vs Strangers

## My Little Rose

Does she see my look,
as she reads her book?
I can't help but stare,
does she know I care?
She is getting so old,
her attitude so bold.
She is growing so fast,
will her innocence last?
Time just whistles by,
and I can't help but sigh.
I watch her sing her song,
and think it won't be long.
Since five she's been mine,
now she's almost nine.
We still have ten years,
before we face our fears.
Did we raise her right,
even when we fight?
I want to do my best,
even when she's a pest.
Will she hate me later,
if I refuse to cater?
I just want her to be smart,
so she'll be safe when we part.
They all grow up and go,
that we all know.
But when she looks back,
will she forgive where I lack?
My love runs so deep,
our memories I will keep.
She is my little rose,
and I'm the mom she chose!

*For Whitnie Bowers*

## My Mother

A lady with a mystery
A woman not many know
She's a person with a gift
She's also got a curse
Surrounded by her walls
All her splendor hidden within
Not many get to see inside
Pain of the past locks her tight
A pillar of strength
She stumbles through life
Looking for something
Which she already has
She feels unloved and alone
Not aware of what's around
You see she is my mother
And I love her so dear
I may not be close by
But my love is always there
I know who she is on the inside
And appreciate all she can be
I thank her for the life she gave me
And will always be hers

## My Dadio

So many things to say
And so little in a way
You know that I love you
No matter what you do
Together no matter what
Even when you're a nut
We are all really one
When it's said and done
But just as you and me
It's all I hoped it'd be
I know we lost some time
But now is 'more than a dime'
Blessed with what we've had
I'm proud you are my dad!

## Lisa's Poem

Even when things look dark,
A prayer can make a spark.
But your belief means more,
Find strength in your core.
Hope alone keeps people alive,
Without it disease can thrive.
Hold onto love in your heart,
It's not time for us to part.
Family will help you be strong,
The new path maybe long.
But that's why we're here,
Don't worry, let go of fear.
We support you all the way,
So we may share another day.

## Serena

Some say she's serene,
During youth I disagreed
We fought most the time
Occasionally partners in crime
Many late nights telling tales
Her tolerance rarely failed
She was my personal slave
Her heart she always gave
She does still to this day
I know her no other way
She's always true to me
Even when I couldn't see
No longer my mini copy cat
Or a little obnoxious brat
A loyal sister she has been
Her last shirt she would lend
I love her with all my heart
No matter how far apart

## Lost in a Moment

Gazing into each others eyes,
forgetting about all those around.
As the words float on the breeze,
they're deaf to any other sound.
Surrounded by peaceful terrain,
the beauty around doesn't compare.
Even divine trees and lake,
couldn't match the loving stare.
Then the phrase we all await,
the moment long overdue.
Hearing you may kiss the bride,
and making it all come true.
*For Serena & Nick*

## **Soul Mate**

If challenges make us close
Then we'll be closer than most
If obstacles build our love
Then we'll have more than enough
If life helps us bond
Then we are one till we're gone
If one things for sure
That is our love is pure
If it's not about the money
Then it's just you and me honey
If we're a team all the way
Then together we'll face the days
If we fight till the end as one
Then our souls have truly won
If pulled apart against our fate
Then I'll wither without my soul mate

*For John Bowers*

*In Loving Memory of Chris Roam*
January 10, 1977 – October 23, 2005

## Our Love

Brought to us as a gift,
taken from us by wings.
As we face our sorrows,
the angels begin to sing.
We pray you found peace,
we hope your soul is free
we know you're still with us,
in our hearts we see.
We cry 'cause we miss you,
we fight to understand.
It hurts that you're not here,
we want to hold your hand.
We know you'll be waiting,
with your arms open wide.
But until we get there,
please stay by our side.

## A New Life for an Old Friend

He was strong like a hammer,
He was solid like a wall.
He was honest with his word,
He was good to us all.
He was clever at NTN,
He was sneaky to log you off.
He was gruff like a bear,
He was loyal and kinda soft.
He was stubborn like an ox,
He was wittier than the best.
He will be missed by many,
He has gone home to rest.
He touched lots of hearts,
Over years from sea to sea.
He chose his own path,
Being who he wanted to be.
He will always be with us,
Each and every day.
He's still watching over Lago,
Just in a different way.

In Memory of Mike "Hammer" Pheland

## A Good Man

Ron Hudlin was a very good man,
his heart as big as the Rio Grande.
Not to forget his contagious smile,
or his laughter shared many a mile.
There's joy in knowing he's free of pain,
but sadness still sheds tears like rain.
Why be down when he's at peace?
Because missing him will never cease.
As he watches from heaven above,
we want him to know how much he is loved.

*In Memory of Ron Hudlin*

---

## In Memory of Jenn Nichols:

Her hair shined like the sun,
and her smile beamed to match.
Those lucky to know her,
she was quite the catch.
She had a heart of gold,
her laughter so full of love.
May her spirit soar high,
to the angels arms above.

Made in the USA
San Bernardino, CA
22 March 2014